IONA

Text by E. Mairi MacArthur

Photography by Colin Baxter

Colin Baxter Photography Ltd., Grantown-on-Spey, Scotland

*An aerial view of Iona, from the north-west. To the left lies the ragged tip of
the Ross of Mull and on the far horizon are the pale blue outlines of Colonsay and Jura.*

Eilean I nan sìthean uaine,
bidh na bàird gu bràth a' luaidh air.

Song by John Campbell, 1905-1999

'Iona of the green hills', an islander wrote, 'poets will forever
sing her praises'. And this they have done, down the ages.

The great Argyll bard Duncan Bàn MacIntyre called the
island 'ionad naomha', a saintly place honoured in lands
far and wide. For William Wordsworth it was 'the Glory of
the West'.

In Gaelic Iona is I Chaluim Chille – the isle of Columcille,
the Irish priest of royal blood who was to become revered as
St Columba. He too was celebrated in praise poetry of enduring
beauty, some of it the earliest surviving literature in the Gaelic
language. In many lines Columba was likened to a bright candle,
a flame that guided and inspired.

So too does Iona itself kindle the imagination of countless
visitors. Small it may be but its historical and spiritual significance
is very great indeed. People have come and gone from its shores
over millennia: pilgrims and warriors, kings and travellers, and
settlers who came to live and so helped create its story.

Small islands often bring to mind gemstones, their patchwork
of rock and turf and sand set amid the spray and sparkle of salt
water. This little book offers a brief insight into what has made
Iona special to so many for so long; a few reflections on this
place of light and colour.

Crystal-clear waters on Iona's western
coast, calm in the summer sunshine,
display a palette of iridescent blues
and greens.

tindis a ainm amail gréin,
ba lés i comair cach oín.
His name glistened like the sun;
He was a light before all.

Beccán mac Luigdech, seventh century AD

A rocky hillock stands opposite the great west door of Iona Abbey. Clumps of daffodils brighten its slopes in spring. Centuries ago someone toiled up its path to a cobbled platform at the top to erect a cross – a sign that this had once been a special spot. It is named Tòrr an Aba (the Abbot's Knoll) and the abbot thus commemorated may well have been the first. Columba's biographer Adomnán, the ninth abbot, implied that the saint's wooden writing hut stood on raised ground close to the monastery.

Adomnán tells us too that, in the 34 years Columba spent as 'an island soldier', many of his days were devoted to prayer and vigil, to reading and writing and the copying of psalms. He will have sat here often, then, this Irishman trained in the skills of war as well as the scholarship of religion. At the age of 42 he had set off across the water to the land now called Argyll, where his Gaelic-speaking countrymen – the Dál Riata – had begun to put down roots. Exactly what motivated this journey in the year AD 563 is shrouded in myth, but choosing to leave home for a far-off place was a recognised tradition in the early Irish church. It was called 'white martyrdom'.

From the knoll Columba could see his monastery clustered

Once collected by local people
to dye wool for weaving, crotal –
a form of lichen – splashes
vivid patterns on a rock face.

St Martin's Cross stands sentinel
between the Street of the Dead,
in the foreground, and the great
west door of Iona Abbey (opposite).

Croft holdings laid out in the early nineteenth century now skirt the Abbey buildings, site of Columba's monastery. Clouds tip the Paps of Jura to the south-east, across the low-lying Ross of Mull and the island of Erraid.

below. This fertile stretch of raised beach on the island's eastern rim had already sheltered waves of prehistoric settlers. Stone-Age farmers left behind a few tools and traces of the crops they tilled. In a stone kerb-cairn, now long grassed over, some Bronze Age mourners buried their dead. It may have been Iron Age inhabitants who built the low earthen rampart, which the monks adapted to provide their curved boundary wall. A portion of this wall still runs north from Sruth a' Mhuillin (the mill-stream).

For their simple wooden buildings, the newcomers may have cleared the last of the oak and ash, birch and hazel that once grew on Iona, although they also had to bring willow for the guest-house from nearby Mull or the mainland. Later, timber was towed some distance to meet the settlement's expanding needs. There was a large hut, warmed by a fire, where the monks lived together, a kitchen, workshops for shoe-maker and wood-turner, a barn to store grain and maybe a herb garden. Columba slept in his own cell with only the bare rock, we are told, as his pillow.

At the centre of this busy community was the little church where the clang of a handbell punctuated the day, calling the brothers to worship. From here Columba's voice, unusually strong and clear, rang out so that every word of the psalms he sang could be heard near and far. On a still day, a shout from across the Sound would warn the monks that a boat was needed for a visitor. One such was so eager to greet the abbot on the knoll that the hem of his clothing knocked over the ink-horn; Columba had both heard the man's call and foretold his clumsiness.

This power of prophecy was one attribute that enhanced the reputation of such a leading figure in the early church. Miracles and angelic visions added strength and sanctity to his cult. Retelling Columba's first miracle when, as a young man in Ireland, he had changed water into wine, Adomnán asked that the story 'shine like a lantern' on all that followed. The tales themselves are full of references to dazzling light, up to the very end of Columba's life. A heavenly glow suffused the church on Iona as the monks ran to find their founding father praying there for the last time, on the night of 9 June 597. At the time of his death, fishermen in Ireland claimed to see a pillar of brilliant fire blaze in the dark sky.

On his last evening Columba climbed a little hill and blessed Iona. Small though it was, he said, the island would be much honoured, by both rulers and peoples at home and abroad and by

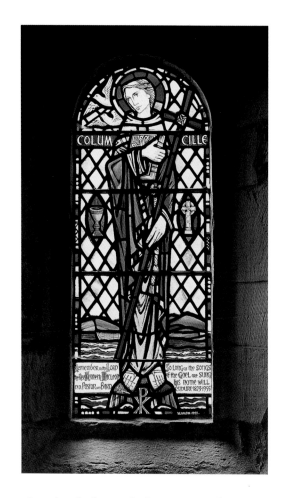

A stained glass window portraying St Columba, designed by William Wilson for the restored north transept of the Abbey in 1965.

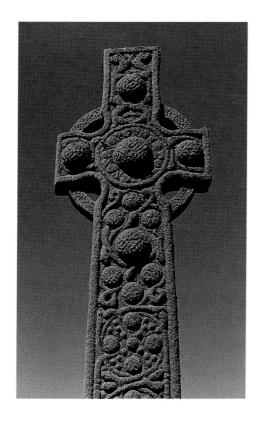

Serpent and boss relief carving on the east face of St Martin's Cross. Of grey epidiorite, it stands staunch and tall in its original base of red granite. One of a group of crosses erected in the late eighth century, close to the early monastic church.

the saints of other churches. As the monastic family of Iona matured, it did indeed attain great stature and became the hub of a lively and inspirational network, with strong links to daughter-houses elsewhere in Argyll and back in Ireland. Succeeding generations of Columban monks probed north into Pictland and east towards Northumbria. A stream of pilgrims found their way to Iona, seeking learning or healing, refuge or absolution. Its very soil was considered hallowed.

One tangible legacy from this era is that of art and sculpture. Iona harbours an outstandingly rich collection of early Christian carved slabs and pillow-stones. A few inscriptions allow us to imagine real people among the ghosts of a distant past: Fergus, Eogan and Flann for whose souls a prayer was requested; 'lapis echodi', the stone of Echoid, a name that appears in the list of those who accompanied Columba to Iona but recurs too among early kings of the Dál Riata.

Around the eighth century skilled masons began to hew magnificent, free-standing crosses. These pictures in stone still fascinate today. Intricate spiral-work and serpents – symbols of eternity – weave marvellous patterns; strange creatures encircle carved bosses; miniature musicians play harp and pipe; mother and child sit shielded by angels. Several of the motifs find an echo in that other artistic glory bequeathed by the early monks, their illuminated manuscripts. A replica of the most celebrated, the Book of Kells, is on display inside the Abbey. For it was very probably on Iona that a team of scribes and illustrators patiently created this exquisite masterpiece.

The Book of Kells is a copy of the Four Gospels, contained in 340 surviving folios, each about 33 x 25 cm (13 x 10 inches). This page (fol. 8r) comes from Matthew. Details of spiral ornamentation, and the depiction of Virgin and Child, find close parallels on Iona's early crosses. Some scholars suggest that the book was made to mark the enshrining of Columba's bones, about AD 750. Some time in the early ninth century it was transferred to the new Columban Monastery at Kells in Ireland. A later annalist described the manuscript as 'the most precious object in the western world'. In its final home, at Trinity College Dublin, the richly jewelled vellum still captivates eye and soul across twelve centuries.

Folio reproduced with the kind permission of the Board of Trinity College, Dublin.

The twin bays of Port an Fhir-Bhreige (port of the false man),
in the foreground, and Port a' Churaich (port of the currach) beyond.
Tradition has long linked this spot with the arrival of Columba.

...*this little island on the edge of the ocean*

Adomnán, *Life of Columba*, III 23

On a sweep of shingle in the south-east corner of Iona the waves
hiss back and forth over shifting layers of multi-coloured
pebbles: yellow and rose-pink, violet and white and dove-grey.
Most prized are those flecked with translucent green serpentine;
the tiniest of them are called, by some, 'St Columba's tears'.

This is Port a' Churaich, which means 'port of the currach',
and a long mound at the head of the beach does resemble an
upturned boat. Perhaps this natural feature gave the bay its name.
A few even used to believe that the saint's vessel was buried there,
until a little digging revealed only earth and rubble. But this whole
area is steeped in Columban lore. A cairn on a nearby hill is linked
with him, for Cùl ri Eirinn ('back towards Ireland') was a poetic
nickname for the saint himself, coined in medieval times. Larger
pebble cairns on the upper beach have kept their own secret over
many centuries, as their origins are unknown. Were they created by
pilgrims wishing to remember or by penitents hoping to forget?

The long-standing tradition that this was where Columba first
landed does make sense to those who know the sea, for the
ebb-tide runs south through the Sound of Iona. The crew of a
hide-and-wicker boat, edging out from the shelter of the Ross of
Mull, might well have thought better of struggling any farther
north just then. It might even have seemed that they would pass
Iona by if the current threatened to drive them out beyond its

*A kaleidoscope of pebbles tumbled
smooth by a silvery sea.*

Looking south-east across Culbhuirg farmland to the rolling, fertile Machair beyond.

Atlantic coast. But at the rocks that divide Port a' Churaich from its twin, Port an Fhir-Bhreige (port of the false man), the tide reverses. It would have been relatively easy to scrape the currach ashore there and wait for the tide to turn.

Columba had first visited Conall, ruler of the kingdom already well established by Scots from Ireland, and who shared his kinsman's Christian faith. Their meeting may have been on the Kintyre peninsula or perhaps at the fort of Dunadd in mid Argyll. It was from there that Columba and his twelve companions continued their voyage to an island destination that King Conall himself may have suggested. The waters of the west were a busy highway in those days; the new Scots will have explored their territory well and a new outpost, from which to press their influence farther north, would have been an attractive notion.

That Iona was also a good place to live must have been obvious as the next flood-tide carried the currach up the eastern side of the island. Perhaps some of the younger monks elected to strike inland on foot. Breasting the slow incline of the Sliabh Siar (western moorland) they will have found at their feet the swathe of green that spans the centre. Here, on the sandy turf called 'machair', the varied strands of Iona's story weave together. Adomnán called this 'the little western plain' where the monks planted and harvested crops. Long rigmarks snaking to the shore are witness to continuing cultivation by the local population from the late middle ages. In the middle of the nineteenth century most of it became the common grazing for nearby crofters.

There was play too, as well as work. Shinty was fiercely

contested here on New Year's Day, giving way to football and, by the 1920s, to a golf match. Nowadays a summer golf competition is equally popular, bringing visitors and locals together. Older folk recall dancing to pipes or fiddle on a summer's evening and they say that music from another, enchanted world might also be heard inside Sìthean Mòr (big fairy mound).

Faith and folklore have long intertwined at this little hill, smooth as green velvet. For on the feast day of St Michael the islanders used to race their horses around it – in the direction of the sun, an echo of pagan ritual. Yet Adomnán had called the same spot 'Cnoc nan Aingeal, that is the angels' knoll', after a radiant heavenly host appeared there, to converse with Columba.

From the sea-cliffs at the south end of the Machair, if tide and swell are right, you may hear a dull boom and catch sight of a plume of spray shooting skywards. Spouting Cave is on show. Below your feet, in summer, the turf is starred with a mass of bright, short-stemmed flowers, genetically adapted to survive centuries of salt breezes and browsing cattle. You can pick out the pink and blue of stork'sbill and milkwort or the yellow blaze of bird's-foot-trefoil; and tread miniature carpets of purple thyme.

Flower-rich fields border the Machair, along the island's western shore.

The modern replica of St John's Cross casts a guardian shadow onto the early chapel now called St Columba's Shrine. This magnificent eighth-century cross has a span wider than any other in Britain or Ireland. The original is housed in the Abbey Museum.

Iona or Icolmkill...
rich in the most interesting antiquities

Letter from John Keats, 1818

Below Tòrr an Aba the scenes shifted and new
casts of characters came on stage as the centuries
rolled by. The wood and wattle cells were replaced
by stone buildings. Scholarship flourished, a library
grew up and important historical annals were
begun. Adomnán, in particular, won lasting esteem
for Iona through his missionary work, his learning
and above all his 'Law of the Innocents', enacted in AD 697 to
protect women, children and clergy from violence and war. To
him also was sainthood later accorded.

The people's toil over many centuries
is etched in deep green furrows below
Dun Bhuirg, an Iron-Age fort on
the west side of the island.

But island monasteries were vulnerable during the troubled
times of the early ninth century, when Viking raiders swept from
the north. In 804 Abbot Cellach began to build Kells in Ireland
as a place of safety for his Iona community, along with their
precious books and relics. Gradually the core of Columban
influence swung back to Ireland. In 849 the bones of the saint
were divided and carried away to Kells, and to the new foundation
of Dunkeld, in central Scotland. Only the tradition of Columba's
grave site lingered on, focused around the tiny chapel that juts
out beside the present Abbey's main door. Over the years it has
become known as St Columba's Shrine.

Around 1200, however, spiritual life on Iona was revitalised

15

A farmer's harvest waits to be brought in alongside the walls of the Benedictine Abbey, now fully restored to its former glory.

with the foundation by Reginald, Lord of the Isles, of a Benedictine abbey dedicated to St Columba. First there rose up a simple, cruciform church. In the course of the century cloisters, dormitories and refectory were built alongside and boatmen were kept busy towing slabs of grey chlorite schist from Knapdale in south Argyll, pale yellow sandstone from the cliffs of Carsaig in Mull and red granite from Eilean nam Bàn just across the Sound of Iona. Major rebuilding in the fifteenth century included the addition of the square tower, ever since a familiar landmark on the island skyline.

The local people called the grand new edifice *an eaglais mhòr*, 'the great church', and no doubt they joined visiting pilgrims there on feast days or to view the relics, central to a medieval abbey's role. The MacDonald history contained in the *Book of Clanranald* tells us that one of their fifteenth-century chiefs gave to Iona 'a covering of gold and silver for the relic of the hand of

Columba'. Through the Middle Ages the secular population had their own parish priest also, with whom they celebrated mass in a small chapel dedicated to St Ronan. This stood close by the Augustinian Nunnery where Beathag, sister of Reginald MacDonald the founder, had come as first prioress.

The Nunnery became known as *an eaglais dhubh*, 'the black church', and the dark-robed sisters walked their own quiet cloister, read and prayed and, as the brothers were doing a short distance away, filed into their church day and night to chant the Latin psalter.

The well-maintained remains of the Nunnery make an attractive, peaceful precinct. Stone and grass today mark out the former chapter-house, cloister-garth and chapel.

The rest of the time, the nuns and monks and the lay servants who helped them – working the land, tending beasts, giving hospitality to guests – will have conversed most commonly in Gaelic. Many of the place-names that enrich the island's landscape may well date from this period. Blàr nam Manach, 'plain of the monks', rises from the Machair and Buaile nan Cailleach may mean 'cattle-fold of the veiled women'. Just beyond there, the Nunnery owned the pasture that slopes south of the Gàradh Dubh Staonaig (black dyke of the inclining ground) – probably the oldest surviving boundary wall on the island. Individuals commemorated on the ground might have

A quiet moment in the Abbey cloister. New carvings of flowers and foliage on the sandstone columns complement the only intact original pair.

Promise of an Easter Day service to come, as evening falls on the choir stalls and marble communion table of the Abbey Church (opposite).

lived at any period, it is true, but it is tempting to wonder if the Marjorie whose enclosure, the Gàradh Marsali, lies just north of the Nunnery once lived within its precincts.

During the Benedictine period, a distinguished school of sculpture flowered on the island, as did others elsewhere in Argyll: in Lorn and Kintyre and on Oronsay. Again, therefore, Iona was part of a wider artistic movement. The masons who built the flowing arches inside the Abbey church, and carved rich detail into their columns, are largely unknown – save for one who literally left his mark. 'Donald O Brolchán', an inscription reads in Latin, 'made this work'. Many of the memorial stones, however, are named and bring to life some of the personalities who shaped those times. Some make clear how interlinked were the worlds of the church and the West Highland aristocracy. Abbot John MacKinnon, for example, was son of a clan chief Lachlan. Four priors came from the one family, believed to be Campbell: John, Patrick and two named Hugo. There is a Mariota, granddaughter of Lachlan, lord of Coll, who became a nun; and one of the last prioresses, Anna Maclean, is poised beautifully in effigy, angels at her pillow, lapdogs peeking out from below her long cloak. Impressive graveslabs to chieftains include those for Colum, son of Ruairi MacLeod, John MacIan lord of Ardnamurchan and Angus MacDonald, son of the lord of Islay. A late addition to these illustrious dead, in 1657, was John Beaton, physician to the clan Maclean and famed in the Highlands as *an t-Ollamh Muileach*, the Mull doctor.

At least nine cemetery sites have been identified on Iona, some of them for specific purposes. Until the late 1700s it was the custom to bury women and children in the Nunnery grounds and the skilled stone-carvers of medieval times were laid to rest at Cladh nan Druinneach (burial ground of the cunning workmen) near Martyrs Bay. This attractive sandy bay has long associations with the rituals of death. Its older name was Port nam Marbh (port of the dead) and it was the traditional landing-place for boats bearing coffins of kings and chiefs, and indeed of native islanders brought home for burial. They were rested

The fresh colours of early summer, looking north across the crofting landscape of Traighmor and Sligineach.

on a small mound before their final journey, along Sraid nam Marbh (the street of the dead) to the Reilig Odhráin.

There is no record of an 'Oran' among the first monks on Iona. And the historical roots of this cemetery's name are now forever misted over by the much later – but darkly popular – legend that Oran volunteered to be buried alive when Columba asked for this supreme sacrifice in order to consecrate the ground. Probably one of the earliest places of Christian burial on the island, it has been the longest in continuous use. Its status was high enough to hold the bones of some early kings – Scots, Irish, Norse – although how many is impossible to say, so unreliable are the written sources. A simple granite stone cut with a single cross is linked with a forgotten king or nobleman from France. The late twelfth-century St Oran's Chapel, typically Irish in plan and decoration, is the oldest of Iona's church sites to survive. It was principally used for family burials by the MacDonald Lords of the Isles through to the fifteenth century.

The Reformation passed peaceably on Iona, owing to the sympathetic leanings of the Bishops of the Isles who were based for a brief period on the island. The monastic community dwindled and the ecclesiastical lands were signed away, bit by bit, to the Macleans of Duart. They in turn had to cede to the increasingly powerful Campbells of Argyll towards the end of the seventeenth century. Iona's inhabitants were by then of Protestant denomination and the ancient buildings fell into decay.

It was to be a long time, however, before the people would have either a new parish church or a resident minister. Until then formal services were held only four times a year, in a house, by a minister from Mull. Yet several early travellers to Iona report that the islanders remained devout and that they would gather on a Sunday inside the crumbling walls of their 'great church', and at the traditional site of their saint's grave, to worship in their own way. Columba's isle was, for a time, bereft of spiritual leadership. It was the ordinary local people who, over at least two centuries, sought out the places sacred to the many generations before them and kept the lamp of faith lit.

Sunset over Soa, an islet due south of Iona, where seals bask and seabirds nest.

The view north from the slopes of Dun I. Towards the top left,
the low dark shape of Staffa is just visible against the misty headlands of Mull.

*It is a very fertile island
and the people are industrious.*

James Boswell, 1773

Iona's highest hill, Dun I, rises only 101 m (332 feet) above sea-level, yet it offers a superb view of the whole island. To the south and west stretches the hummocky landscape formed by grey rocks called Lewisian Gneiss which, at 2800 million years old, are among the most ancient on Earth. So old are they, in fact, that no fossils are to be found here. Its geology too thus makes Iona distinctive, a clear contrast with the much younger mass of red granite just a mile across the water on the Ross of Mull. Boulders of this granite are strewn profusely along Iona's shoreline, tossed at random by retreating ice-sheets at the end of the Ice Ages. A huge one is even perched high on the slopes of Dun I. Many of these erratic blocks were split and worked by local stonemasons in years gone by, to find a permanent home on Iona in dwellings, byres and walls.

To the north, fringes of dazzling white sand meet shallow coastal waters of pale emerald and aquamarine, shading into intense blue. Small wonder this has been one of the most painted locations in Scotland. In the 1920s and '30s it was a favourite spot for artists such as Cadell, Peploe and Hunter, who now command a worldwide reputation as members of the Scottish Colourists.

Island landscapes can be fragile, open as they are to the relentless pressure of wind and sea. National Trust for Scotland

Once the mainstay of the local economy, cattle are still reared by several of the island's crofters and farmers.

23

Across the Sound of Iona, the terraced cliffs of Burg rise above Kentra point and, behind them, Mull's highest peak, Ben More, is wreathed in cloud.

volunteers have planted marram grass along the dunes, as the crofters themselves used to do, to stem erosion and conserve the outstanding beauty of these beaches. The scene was not always so peaceful. In one of the Viking attacks, the story goes, Iona's brethren were slain where they stood on Tràigh Bàn nam Manach, ever after named 'fair strand of the monks'.

On and around Dun I are reminders of local custom and celebration. Near the summit is a rock pool called Tobar na h-Aois (well of age). Bathe your face three times here as the sun rises and your youth will be magically restored. The cairn was built in 1897 to mark Queen Victoria's Diamond Jubilee and a bonfire was lit, as was the tradition, by the oldest resident. A boggy area on the lower slopes of the hill is remembered as Lòn a' Phoit Dhubh – 'meadow of the black pot' – where the whisky still might quickly be hidden from the eyes of the exciseman.

A popular spot with walkers is a simple stone circle at Cobhan Cuilteach, literally 'secluded hollow'. Many like to call it Hermit's Cell, believing that it started out as a beehive-shaped hut where monks could spend times of quiet contemplation. Even today, birdsong is often the only sound on the air. Later, perhaps, the local girls brought their cattle into the circle for milking from the rugged hill pasture nearby. The neat pattern of arable fields visible from Dun I dates from 1802 when individual holdings, or crofts, were first created. Visitors had long remarked on Iona's good agricultural land. Boswell, Dr Johnson's travelling companion in 1773, was impressed by the self-sufficiency of the local population, then around 250; they grew or made everything for themselves, he noted, save salt and iron.

By the mid nineteenth century, however, numbers had spiralled upwards to over 500 and poor harvests or low prices for cattle regularly threatened livelihoods. Worst of all was 1846, known in Gaelic as 'a' bhliadhna a dh' fhalbh am buntàta' – the year the potato went away – when blight struck that staple crop. Years of hunger, debt and emigration followed.

By the close of the century the population had stabilised at around 200. The growing number of summer visitors, who stayed in the two hotels, rented houses and hired boats, brought in vital extra money. All year the institutions of community life remained strong: concerts, sports days and regattas, debates in the schoolhouse, spinning of yarns at the smiddy. Central to parish life was weekly worship in one of two places, either the United Free Church, perched since 1849 on the curve of Martyrs Bay, or the Church of Scotland, designed by Thomas Telford in 1828 and built on an ancient chapel site dedicated to Cainnech (St Kenneth), a close friend of Columba.

Eddies swirl in alongside the pier while rainy squalls threaten from the south. The former United Free Church is silhouetted against hill and sky.

Morning light bathes the village houses, clustered around the island's principal landing place at Port Rònain.

Ach mun tig an saoghal gu crìch, bidh I mar a bha.
But ere the world come to an end,
Iona shall be as it was.

Anonymous saying

Iona's deserted monuments were deeply impressive to eighteenth-
and nineteenth-century visitors. Even to stand among the ruins,
claimed Dr Johnson, would stir the embers of piety in any heart.

And in 1899 a new era opened. The 8th Duke of Argyll gifted
all the ecclesiastical sites to a new public body, the Iona
Cathedral Trust, with the express wish that the Abbey Church be
rebuilt and open to all faiths for worship. By 1910 this had been
completed. The first island wedding had already been held there
and the local congregation gathered often within the restored
walls, for regular services and large special events. To mark
St Columba's Day in June 1936, a Gaelic service was broadcast
from Iona Abbey for the first time, conducted by the parish
minister. He took as his text *solus an t-Soisgeul* (the light of the
Gospel) that had come to the island, and gone forth again, with
the saint.

From the high soaring window at the east end of the choir,
light streams down on a slab of Iona marble, formed into a
handsome communion table. It takes the place of the medieval
altar, long since broken into pieces by the superstitious, seeking
cures for illness. The marble quarry operated briefly in the
1790s and again for a few years from 1907 when the distinctive

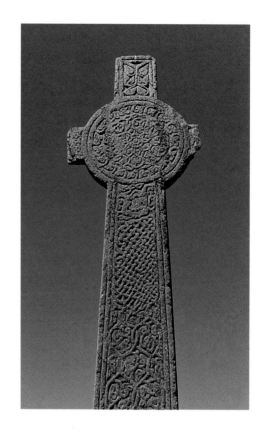

*The east side of the fifteenth-century
Maclean's Cross, its finely wrought
carving testifying to the skill
of Iona's past craftsmen.*

The Abbey Church viewed from the north with its domestic complex where the monks slept, ate and studied. Farthest to the left was the medieval infirmary, now the Abbey Museum.

green-veined stone was in great demand. White marble from Carrara was the choice of sculptor Sir George Frampton, whose effigies of the 8th Duke of Argyll and his third wife lie in the south transept.

In the summer of 1938 a long wooden hut was erected in the shadows of the Abbey walls, heralding the final scenes on the stage where Columba's monks first delved into the earth. Plans to rebuild the rest of the monastic complex had been mooted by many people over several decades. The one that came to fruition was the brainchild of the Revd George F. MacLeod, whose ministry in urban areas during the Depression years had convinced him that the Church needed a fresh vision. He brought young ministers to Iona, to work alongside joiners and builders so that spiritual and physical renewal might be seen to work hand in hand. This was the start of the Iona Community.

By 1965 their ambitious restoration programme was complete, blending new with old. The flowers and birds of Iona adorn the reconstructed columns in the cloister. White doves flutter from the medieval doocot in the tower. Guests from all over the world share meals with Iona Community staff and volunteers in the bright, airy refectory, lit by four original windows and under a modern roof of Norwegian timber. Across the road, the MacLeod Centre was opened in 1988 to cater especially for families, youth groups and disabled visitors.

The cap-house on the Abbey tower, an original feature of the medieval building, was replaced in 1996 by the local work squad then employed by the Iona Cathedral Trust. In April 2000, the Trust's responsibilities for managing and maintaining all the ecclesiastical sites were transferred to Historic Scotland. In its care are the Abbey, St Oran's Chapel, the Nunnery, Maclean's Cross and all the carved stones and slabs. A magnificent selection of these is on display in a small museum to the north-east of the Abbey. Historic Scotland also tends the ancient graveyard, used to this day by the local people and a place for quiet personal remembrance.

The daily worship of the Iona Community is ecumenical and open to all. In addition, Church of Scotland services are held weekly in the parish church and a little chapel is attached to the Bishop's House, a guest-house built in 1894 and still run by the Episcopal Church in Scotland. The Roman Catholic Church used

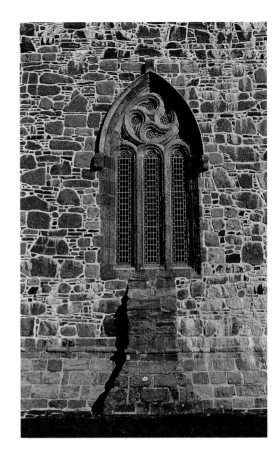

A colourful mosaic of stonework, medieval and modern, frames a window in the south transept of Iona Abbey.

A focal point for islanders and visitors alike. Behind, the regular ferry from Fionnphort approaches the pier while one of the boats for Staffa waits at the slipway.

to organise huge pilgrimages, bringing hundreds by special steamer to celebrate mass in the open air. In 1996 the Colmcille Trust, a new charitable body, opened a specially dedicated guest-house with its own small oratory in which to welcome visitors of the Catholic faith.

For many, therefore, Iona remains first and foremost 'The Sacred Isle', a term in common use since the days of tours on foot or horseback, by sailing skiff or steamship. A wellspring of religious faith, such as this, retains a strong pull. But among the thousands who spill off the modern car ferry every year are some who come for other reasons too. The island's geological interest is considerable and this in turn has contributed to a range of natural habitats, favouring a rich variety of Hebridean plant and bird life. Oyster-catcher and sandpiper scuttle along the shoreline, its rocks pink with sea-thrift; in early summer a few corncrakes, now rare, rasp insistently from deep inside stands of yellow flag-iris. An ideal place for a peaceful holiday, Iona has attracted many who have become regulars, returning year after year and forming lasting ties of friendship. Children come to stay with grandparents, natives who left young return to visit relatives, descendants of emigrants seek their family roots.

For Iona is not merely a museum of sites and scenery. Its fame stems primarily from the people who have lived there and who, in various ways, have placed its life on record. Iona's written history first came alive through the skilful pen of Adomnán, enshrining Columba's reputation forever. Much about the religious past and present may be gleaned directly from the stones and crosses, the restored buildings and the activities of the different church communities. The islanders' own history is displayed in the Heritage Centre. Each generation that passes leaves lines on the landscape, memories in the place-names, narratives for the re-telling.

The history of Iona is a long and colourful one, although sombre shades have tinged many chapters of its people's tale. Island life is never easy, in any age. As that story unfolds into the future it continues to be interpreted, in word and picture. Writers and poets try to evoke Iona's special atmosphere. Painters seek to recreate on canvas the elusive hues of land, sea and sky. And the camera's eye captures moments, in the ever-changing light.

The sea road to Iona, plied over thousands of years. On it there have come learning and piety, culture and community and livelihood, hardship and very real peril – but also great hope and new life.